SAYING GOODBYE TO A PET

written by Cash Allen

illustrated by Terry Allen

Ashland Ink

Saying Goodbye to a Pet
Copyright ©2024 by Cash Allen
Copyright illustrations ©2024 by Terry Allen
Author: Cash Allen
Illustrator: Terry Allen

Published by Ashland Ink Publishing
209 West 2nd Street #177
Fort Worth TX 76102
www.ashlandink.com

Published in the United States of America

ISBN: 978-1-963514-06-3 (hardback)
ISBN: 978-1-963514-05-6 (paperback)

Dedicated to my mom,
Anna Allen

Guess how much I love animals?
Soooooo much!

At my house we have one dog,
one parakeet and a fish.

But we got my first pet
before I was even born.
She was already 8 years old!

She was a little black cute
dog named Scout.

How adorable!

She liked to roll around making funny sounds
to make me laugh.

She would sleep and cuddle with me when I was sick.

She was small...

but so brave, courageous and bold
around big dogs.

She

REALLY

LOVED

ice cream.

Eventually she was
10 years old...

then even 15 years old!

It was hard for her to hear and see us.

SCOUT!!!

Then one day I came home from school.
I was hanging out and being happy.
But then my parents walked in and we talked.
They said Scout was very sick. And we were
going to have to put her down.

That meant she ONLY HAD SEVEN DAYS MORE LEFT TO LIVE!!

I got very sad.

"THIS IS THE WORST
DAY EVER!" I SAID.

My mom said we would love her and spoil her before she had to go to the vet.
So we gave her lots of pets and hugs and kisses and treats.

We got to sleep in bed together.
Our other dog Rigby felt jealous.

The one day came,
the day Scout went to the vet.

My mom said, "the vet
will put a shot in her arm
and she will fall asleep".

If you wonder if it will hurt, I had the same question.

IT WILL NOT HURT.

We gave Scout a
chocolate hug and kiss.

(Not recommended
for healthy "doggos")

The vet came in and we had a little chit-chat. Then she had the shot. She was sticking her tongue out one inch. It was funny and sad.

We gave her our last hugs and
kisses and cuddles.
Everyone cried - especially my Mom.

We got her paw print in a week.
We look at it to remember the great time
we've had with her.

The end.

ABOUT THE AUTHOR

Cash Allen is 7 years old and lives with his family in Texas. He's a Cub Scout, piano player and swimmer. He loves school, and animals of all kinds. When he grows up he wants to be a veterinarian and author.

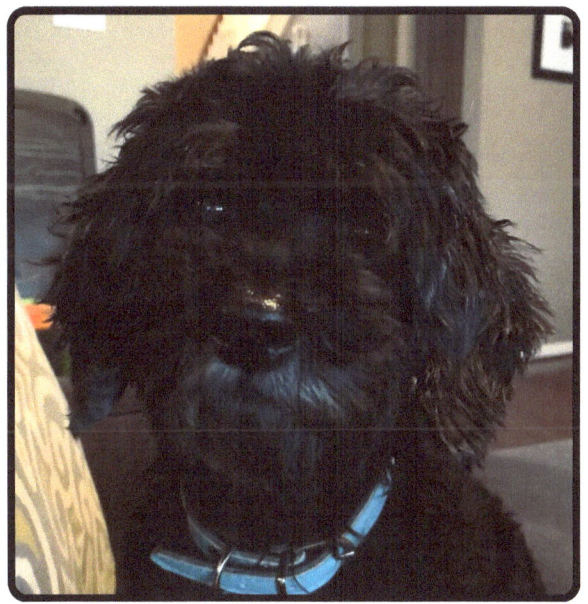

www.ingramcontent.com/pod-product-compliance
Lightning Source LLC
LaVergne TN
LVHW072059070426
835508LV00002B/183